VETERINARIANS
A First Look

PERCY LEED

GRL Consultant, Diane Craig, Certified Literacy Specialist

Lerner Publications ◆ Minneapolis

Educator Toolbox

Reading books is a great way for kids to express what they're interested in. Before reading this title, ask the reader these questions:

What do you think this book is about? Look at the cover for clues.

What do you already know about veterinarians?

What do you want to learn about veterinarians?

Let's Read Together

Encourage the reader to use the pictures to understand the text.

Point out when the reader successfully sounds out a word.

Praise the reader for recognizing sight words such as *for* and *at*.

TABLE OF CONTENTS

Veterinarians. 4

Veterinarians

Veterinarians are animal doctors. They are also called vets.

stethoscope

Vets know how animal bodies work.

They use tools to check on animals.

otoscope

Why do vets check animals' ears?

Animals cannot talk.
Vets test animals to
find out what hurts.

Some vets work with big animals.

They may go to farms.

Some vets work with small animals.

They care for pets.
They may give them shots.

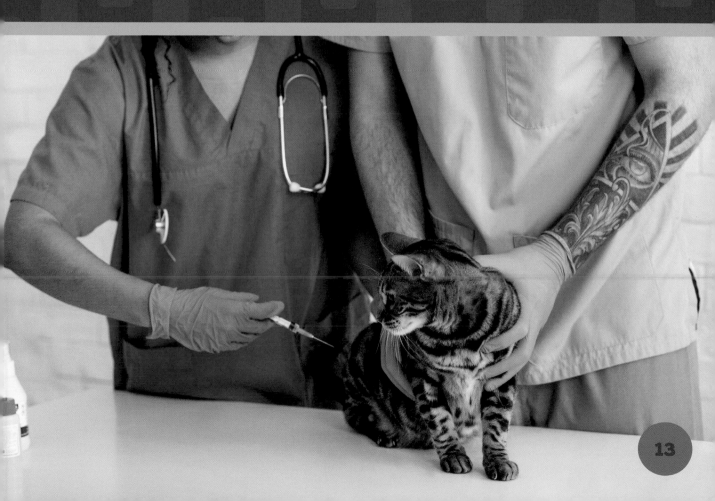

Some vets work
with wild animals.

What kind of animal would you want to help?

Why does going to the vet scare animals?

Animals may get scared at the vet. Vets help them feel safe.

Vets go to school for many years.

Vets work hard to help animals!

You Connect!

What is something you like about veterinarians?

How can a veterinarian help an animal you know?

Would you like to be a veterinarian when you grow up?

Social and Emotional Snapshot

Student voice is crucial to building reader confidence. Ask the reader:

What is your favorite part of this book?

What is something you learned from this book?

Did this book remind you of any community helpers you've met?

Photo Glossary

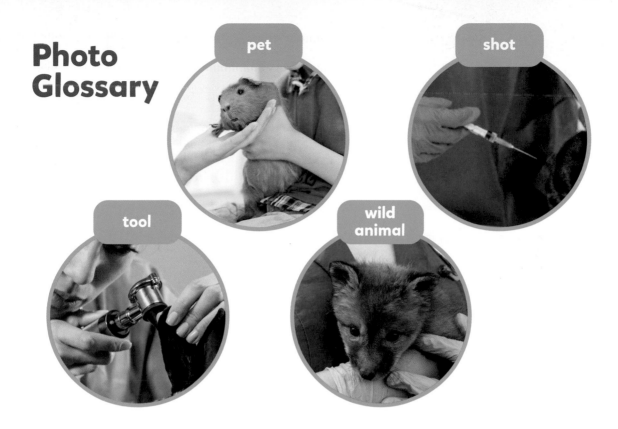

pet

shot

tool

wild animal

Learn More

Katz, Susan B. *All about Veterinarians*. Minneapolis: Lerner Publications, 2023.

Romero, Libby. *Animal Doctors*. Washington, DC: National Geographic Kids, 2023.

Sterling, Charlie W. *A Day with a Veterinarian*. Minneapolis: Jump!, 2022.

Index

Photo Acknowledgments

The images in this book are used with the permission of: © Robert Daly/iStockphoto, pp. 4–5, 23 (top left); © CAP53/iStockphoto, p. 6; © kali9/iStockphoto, pp. 7, 23 (bottom left); © SeventyFour/iStockphoto, pp. 8–9; © PeopleImages/iStockphoto, pp. 10–11; © AnnaStills/iStockphoto, p. 12; © Prostock-Studio/iStockphoto, pp. 13, 23 (top right); © danilobiancalana/Shutterstock Images, pp. 14–15; © ALIAKSANDR PALCHEUSKI/Shutterstock Images, pp. 14, 23 (bottom right); © shironosov/iStockphoto, pp. 16–17; © Igor Alecsander/iStockphoto, pp. 18–19; © Prostock-studio/Shutterstock Images, p. 20.

Cover Photograph: © kali9/iStockphoto

Design Elements: © Mighty Media, Inc.

Lerner Publications Company
An imprint of Lerner Publishing Group, Inc.
241 First Avenue North
Minneapolis, MN 55401 USA

For reading levels and more information, look up this title at www.lernerbooks.com.

Main body text set in Mikado a Medium.
Typeface provided by Hannes von Doehren.

Library of Congress Cataloging-in-Publication Data

Names: Leed, Percy, 1968–author.
Title: Veterinarians : a first look / Percy Leed.
Description: Minneapolis, MN : Lerner Publications Company, [2025] | Series: Read about community helpers | Includes bibliographical references and index. | Audience: Ages 5–8 | Audience: Grades K–1 | Summary: "Veterinarians have a really tough job; their patients can't talk. Animal lovers will enjoy this engaging text with full-color photographs about the people who keep our animals healthy and safe"—Provided by publisher.
Identifiers: LCCN 2023035579 (print) | LCCN 2023035580 (ebook) | ISBN 9798765626474 (library binding) | ISBN 9798765629598 (paperback) | ISBN 9798765637043 (epub)
Subjects: LCSH: Veterinarians—Juvenile literature. | Veterinary medicine—Juvenile literature. | Pets—Health—Juvenile literature.
Classification: LCC SF756 .L44 2025 (print) | LCC SF756 (ebook) | DDC 636.089—dc23/eng/20231212

LC record available at https://lccn.loc.gov/2023035579
LC ebook record available at https://lccn.loc.gov/2023035580

Manufactured in the United States of America
1 – CG – 7/15/24